Facilit

MW01242082

Elephants in the Church
CONVERSATIONS WE CAN'T AFFORD TO IGNORE

BEACON HILL PRESS
OF KANSAS CITY

Elephants in the Church
CONVERSATIONS WE CAN'T AFFORD TO IGNORE

Writer/Editor
Mike L. Wonch
Director of Curriculum
Merritt J. Nielson
Director of Editorial
Bonnie Perry

ISBN: 978-0-8341-2985-6
Printed in U.S.A.

10 9 8 7 6 5 4 3 2 1

TABLE OF CONTENTS

USING THIS FACILITATOR'S GUIDE

The purpose of this facilitator's guide is to help you lead people into community as they grow in Christ by studying the Word.

TAKE A LOOK

1. Before you begin to prepare for the first session, get an overview of the entire study. This will enable you to:

    • Understand the direction of each session and the overall purpose of the study.

    • Know what your group will be reading and studying each week.

    • Begin to think and plan what you would like to accomplish by doing this study.

2. Before you teach each session,

    • Read over your Facilitator's Guide session for that week, several times, prior to your small group meeting. This will help you become familiar with questions, activities, options, and so on.

    • Gather any needed materials.

    • Pray for God's direction.

THE SESSIONS

Each session contains:

    • *Opening our Minds*—the introductory material relevant to the topic for the session.

    • *Opening the Word*—the Bible study portion of the session.

    • *Opening our Hearts*—the opportunity for the group to understand how the truth discovered during the session applies to their lives.

    • *Imaginative Option*—an activity option to bring extra creativity to your session.

    • *Connect*—each week you will have the opportunity to send your class a text and/or email update of what you will study in the upcoming week. We have provided the weekly text for you to use each week and is designed to be sent to your group the week prior to the session. You can use the message provided as is, or feel free to edit and add your own words to meet the needs of your particular group.

INVOLVE EVERYONE

We design the questions and activities to enable everyone to participate. Here are some things to keep in mind as you lead your small group:

1. Adults are more interested when they are participants instead of spectators.
2. They'll remember more of what they discuss and do together than what is said in a lecture.
3. When participants get involved in a discussion, be affirming and encouraging.
4. Don't force anyone to participate, but do make sure everyone knows his or her input is welcome.
5. Relax. Do your homework and don't feel tense about the session. Give your best effort, and let the Lord take care of the rest.
6. Pray for each adult in the session that they will benefit from the study. Pray for yourself that God will assist you as you lead.

ENCOURAGE GROUP MEMBERS . . .

- *To read.* Invite them to read the participant material prior to each session. This allows them to prepare their minds for the topic to be discussed that week.
- *To pray.* This allows them to prepare their hearts for what God wants to show them through the lesson.
- *To be open.* Be open to the lesson, the group members, and especially to God's leading.

CREATING AN ATMOSPHERE OF OPENNESS (HOSPITALITY)

Focus Scriptures: Acts 2:42-47; Romans 12:9-13

Session Goal: To understand the importance of Christian love and hospitality expressed inside and outside the church.

OPENING OUR MINDS

Option 1

Share the following definition of hospitality with your group: *kindness to visitors: friendly, welcoming, and generous treatment offered to guests or strangers.*[1]

Invite your group to think about hospitality. Then ask, **How are people made to feel welcome at the following places?**
—Hotel
—Neighborhood
—School
—Restaurant

- **What do we in the church do to make people feel welcome?**
- **Are there people who, because of their beliefs or lifestyle, might feel unwelcomed by those inside the church? If so, why?**

1. http://www.bing.com/Dictionary/search?q=define+hospitality&qpvt=hospitality +definition+&FORM=DTPDIA Accessed October 1, 2012.

Option 2

Begin by asking your group to think about a time when they were treated unfriendly, unwelcomed, or like a stranger.

- **What things happened, or didn't happen, that made you feel this way?**
- **How did this experience make you feel?**
- **What could have been done to make you feel welcomed and a part of the group?**
- **What did you learn from this experience?**

Then ask,

- **Are there people who we think feel unwelcomed by those inside the church? If so, why?**
- **Because of their lifestyles or opinions, do you think there might be people we, intentionally or unintentionally, treat as "outsiders" or "unwelcomed"?**

Imaginative Option

Bring donuts and coffee to your group. Place a sign on the table, "For right-handed people only!" As group members come in, watch their reaction and listen for their comments. Then begin your group time by discussing what the group thought and felt about the sign. (Be sure everyone gets to enjoy the coffee and donuts.)

- **Are there things we do in the church that might make some people feel left out or unwelcomed?**

OPENING THE WORD

Understanding Acts 2:42-47

In Acts 2 we read of the coming of the Holy Spirit (Pentecost). Peter preached to the crowd gathered, and three thousand came to faith in Christ that day—the church begins. But what happens next? Today's verses give us a glimpse of the early church. These early Christ-followers devoted themselves to the teaching of the apostles. They gathered in fellowship, partaking in the Lord's Supper and praying. They sold their material possessions and gave to the poor and anyone in need. They ate together and praised God. Each day people were added to their numbers.

The characteristics of the early church were fellowship, prayer, worship, praise, and service to others. This is the model for the church of today to follow.

Option 1

Ask your group to think about the church.

- **How would you define the church?**
- **What are the characteristics of the church?**

Read Acts 2:42-47.

- **What are the characteristics of the early church?**
- **Why are teaching, fellowship, the Lord's Supper, prayer, eating together, service to others, and praise and worship important practices for the church?**

Share with the group that early believers had a contagious kind of community. Outsiders were drawn toward their love. Nothing was hidden and everything was shared. The effect this kind of Spirit-filled hospitality had on

CREATING AN ATMOSPHERE OF OPENNESS

people was that *"the Lord added to their number daily those who were being saved"* (Acts 2:47).

- **Why do you think people were drawn to the early church?**
- **What draws people to the church today?**
- **What are the barriers to transparency and authenticity within the body of Christ?**

Option 2

Read Acts 2:42-47. Then write on a dry erase board the following words: teaching, fellowship, Communion, prayer, service, praise. Discuss each word; how it was important for the early church and how important it is for the church today.

- **What are the ways we can reach out to those outside of the church?**
- **What are the ways we can build our relationships with those inside the church?**

Understanding Romans 12:9-13

According to Paul, part of being the church means expressing sincere love, being devoted to one another, serving the Lord, sharing with one another, and practicing hospitality. These characteristics are applied to both those inside and outside the four walls of the church. The Christian life is lived in relationship with God and others.

OPENING OUR HEARTS

Option 1

Read Romans 12:9-13. We are to model the practices of the early church. Part of being the church also means expressing love and hospitality toward others. According to Acts 2:42-47 and Romans 12:9-13:

- **How do we create a genuine environment of openness to others outside the church? How do we create a genuine environment of openness to others inside the church?**

- **How can we enter into spiritual conversations that lead us to a deeper understanding of God and closer walk with Him?**

Ask your group to reflect on their relationship to those outside the church.

- **What is one way you can practice love and hospitality to those outside the church this week?**

Ask your group to reflect on their relationship to those inside the church.

- **What is one way you can practice love and hospitality to those inside the church this week?**

Option 2

Read Romans 12:9-13.

- **What is the overall message of these verses?**

Then read Acts 2:42-47.

- **In what ways do Romans 12:9-13 and Acts 2:42-47 relate to one another?**

Share with the group that the Greek word translated *"hospitality"* in Rom. 12:13 implies offering friendship to strangers. Paul instructed the church to practice hospitality. This was a call to pursue those they weren't already intimately connected to within their circle of fellowship for the purpose of demonstrating the loving friendship offered by God.

- **What is one way you can practice hospitality to those outside the church this week?**
- **What is one way you can practice hospitality to those inside the church this week?**
- **How can we enter into spiritual conversations that lead us to a deeper understanding of God and closer walk with Him?**

Connect -

WEEK I

Creating an Atmosphere of Openness

THIS WEEK: Early believers had an infectious kind of fellowship. Outsiders were drawn within by their love. Nothing was hidden. All was shared. We're told the effect this kind of Spirit-filled hospitality had on people: *"the Lord added to their number daily those who were being saved"* (Acts 2:47). This week we will look at the characteristics of the early church.

THINK ABOUT THIS: How do we unlock the doors of fellowship, creating a genuine environment of openness to others?

PRAYER CONCERNS:

WHEN IS ENOUGH ENOUGH? (MATERIALISM)

Focus Scriptures: Ecclesiastes 5:10; Mark 10:17-23 .

Session Goal: To help students gain a biblical perspective of material possessions.

OPENING OUR MINDS

Option 1

Begin by asking your group to imagine that they have just inherited a *very large* sum of money from a relative. Then, ask them to respond to the following:

- **What would be the first five things you would do with this money?**
- **How would this money change your life?**
- **Would this money make you more or less materialistic?**
- **Would you respond to the needy any differently?**

Follow up by asking the group to consider this question silently to themselves:

- **What would your thoughts and feelings be if you felt God telling you to give the full amount of the inheritance away?**
- **What would your thoughts and feelings be if you felt God telling you to give away your lifesavings?**

Option 2

Most people would agree that they have more "stuff" than they really need, or can even use. Actually, our closets and garages are full of things that are in perfectly good condition, but are no longer used for one reason or another. Have your group think about all the contents in their home. This would include furniture, clothing, lawn equipment, and so on.

Then, ask your group to respond to the following:

- **Name one item in your home you could live without.**
- **Name one item in your home you could not live without.**
- **Think of one item in your home that even though you could, you would not want to live without. What makes this item so important to you?**
- **Do you think people are too attached to their material possessions? Why, or why not?**

Imaginative Option

There are many programs on television that focus on the lifestyles of the wealthy. During these programs we are usually given a tour of their home, shown all the cars they own, and see other material possessions they have acquired that only the rich are able to afford. Show a clip from one these programs. Then, follow up by asking:

- **What makes a program like this so popular?**
- **What is the message of the program?**
- **Do you think people watch this program and wish they had the kind of possessions and lifestyle as the person, or persons, featured?**

OPENING THE WORD

Understanding Ecclesiastes 5:10

It is not known who wrote the book of Ecclesiastes. (Some believe these words might have been written by Solomon, the richest man who ever lived.) Although it is unclear who the author is, it *is* clear that the writer points to the fact that anything less than a life centered on God, especially one consumed with the pursuit of wealth, is meaningless. Wealth and possessions can never satisfy; therefore, only God can satisfy needs of the human heart and life.

Understanding Mark 10:17-23

Jesus was approached by a man. Luke called him a "ruler" and Matthew referred to him as "young." (We refer to him as the "Rich Young Man or Ruler.") Most likely he was part of the elite establishment of the time.

The young man's question of "what must *I* do" indicated he was seeking some list of rules to follow in order to receive eternal life. Jesus' response focused on the commandments concerning people: do not kill, do not commit adultery, do not steal, do not lie, steer clear of defrauding our neighbor, and honor our parents. The man acknowledged that he had kept these commands since childhood. Jesus saw the man's sincerity, but also saw that the man believed external conformity to the law was the key to his relationship with God *and* eternal life. This man was probably a good person and followed the Law faithfully. However, "the one thing he lacked" was his security in his wealth and possessions and not in God. He went away sad because he was not willing to surrender *everything* to follow Christ. The tragedy of this story is that this man's greatest treasure was on earth, not in heaven.

Option 1

Begin by asking:

- **What is the purpose of material possessions?**
- **Is their anything wrong with having material possessions?**
- **Is there anything wrong with being wealthy or financially well-off?**

Read Ecclesiastes 5:10.

- **What are the characteristics of someone who loves money?**
- **What does the author mean by "whoever loves wealth is never satisfied?"**

Read Mark 10:17-23.

- **Despite the fact that the young man had followed the commandments mentioned in verse 19, why did Jesus say he was still lacking something?**
- **Why did Jesus command him to "sell everything and give to the poor?"**
- **Does this command apply to everyone? If not, why?**

Option 2

Read Ecclesiastes 5:10.

- **What is the message of this verse?**

Read Mark 10:17-23.

- **What do you think are the key truths of this story?**

Follow up by asking:

- **What do these Scripture passages say about money and possessions?**
- **Does having money and possessions go counter to the message of the Bible?**
- **What do these Scripture passages have to say to us about those our culture would consider wealthy?**

OPENING OUR HEARTS

Option 1

Read each quote below and ask the group to respond.

"You say, 'If I had a little more, I should be very satisfied.' You make a mistake. If you are not content with what you have, you would not be satisfied if it were doubled." —Charles Haddon Spurgeon

- **What is the key to being content and satisfied with what you have?**

"He is no fool who gives what he cannot keep to gain what he cannot lose." —Jim Elliot

- **What is the key to living simplistically when it comes to material possessions?**

Close by reading Matthew 6:30-33 from *The Message*:

"If God gives such attention to the appearance of wildflowers—most of which are never even seen—don't you think he'll attend to you, take pride in you, do his best for you? What I'm trying to do here is to get you to relax, to not be so preoccupied with getting, so you can respond to God's giving. People who don't know God and the way he works fuss over these things, but you know both God and how he works. Steep your life in God-reality, God-initiative, God-provisions. Don't worry about missing out. You'll find all your everyday human concerns will be met."

Option 2

Ask your group to think about this question silently to themselves: **Do I own my possessions or do my possessions own me?**

There is nothing wrong with having food, clothing, and shelter. However, our perspective on material possessions may be more in line with how culture views "stuff" rather than how God does.

Share the following regarding the danger of material possessions:

- *We may focus too much time on the accumulation of material goods and what others have. This can lead to feelings of greed for more and envy of others' material possessions.*
- *We are more concerned with our own interests rather than the needs of others. This leads to a selfish attitude of "me" before "others."*
- *We view the accumulation of material possessions equivalent to success. This buys in to the lie that the more you have the more you successful you are or appear to be.*
- *We rely more on the power of money than on the power of God for our daily needs. This weakens our faith and trust in God.*

Imaginative Option

Show the *Nooma* video "Kickball." This video deals with trusting God. You can checkout the *Nooma* videos at www.nooma.com.

Connect

WEEK 2

When Is Enough Enough?

THIS WEEK: We all need food, clothing, and shelter. However, what else do we really need to survive? This week we will examine a biblical view of material possessions and a Christian perspective on owning "stuff."

THINK ABOUT THIS: How do I know when enough is enough when it comes to material possessions?

PRAYER CONCERNS:

WEIGHING FACTS WITH OUR THUMB ON THE SCALES (PREJUDICE)

Focus Scripture: James 2:1-13

Session Goal: To help students examine why prejudice exists and ways in which they can overcome prejudice and allow God's grace to flow through their lives.

OPENING OUR MINDS

Option 1

Ask each person in the group to think about a time when they were treated, or judged, unfairly. Invite them to think about their thoughts and feelings regarding this experience then, and now.

Invite volunteers to share their experience using the following questions as a guide to the discussion:

- **What were the circumstances surrounding this situation?**
- **How did this experience make you feel?**
- **What was the result, or outcome, of this situation?**
- **What did you learn from this experience?**
- **Has that experience changed the way you treat others?**

Option 2

According to the dictionary, "prejudice" is *"an opinion formed before hand, usually an unfavorable one based on insufficient knowledge, irrational feelings or inaccurate stereotypes."*[2]

---

2. < http://encarta.msn.com/dictionary_1861737282/prejudice.html>. Accessed June 3, 2008.

Using the definition above, ask the group to give one example of prejudice in action with each of the following:

- **Outward appearance**
- **Religious beliefs**
- **Economic status**
- **Age**
- **Accent**
- **Race**

Follow up by asking:

- **Where does prejudice exist?**
- **Why does prejudice exist?**

Imaginative Option

Obtain the following images: a person with multiple piercings or tattoos, a person with long hair, a homeless person, a wealthy person, and a muscular individual.

Show each image separately and ask people to think about their perception of the image silently to themselves.

- **Where do we get our perception of others?**
- **How do our perceptions of others affect the way we treat them?**
- **Can our perceptions lead to prejudice thoughts and actions? If so, how?**

OPENING THE WORD

Understanding James 2:1-13

God has no favorites, and neither should we as followers of Christ. James was warning early Christians not to show favor and give preferential treatment toward the wealthy because of their economic and social position in society. He used the example of a rich man (a ring and fine clothes signify a person of high social status) and a poor man ("shabby" clothing denotes dirty or filthy type garments) visiting a synagogue. The rich man was given a seat while the poor man was given the floor. Special treatment was given to the rich person because of his social standing and wealth. James makes it clear that this kind of behavior is not in step with the life of Jesus—the One to whom they belong. James warned early Christians not to judge people according to society's standard, but to show mercy as God had shown mercy toward each of them.

Option 1

Begin by asking:

- **How do you define favoritism?**
- **Do you think showing favoritism is the same thing as being prejudiced?**

Read James 2:1-4.

- **Why do you think James used a rich person and a poor person for his example of favoritism?**
- **How did the people's act of favoritism cause them to "become judges with evil thoughts?"**

Read verses 5-11.

- **What is the "royal law?"**
- **Why is favoritism considered a "sin?"**

- Why are those who show favoritism considered "lawbreakers?"

Read verses 12-13.

- How does the "royal law" or the "law of love" bring freedom?
- Why is mercy an important part of the Christian life?
- How does mercy triumph over judgment?

Follow up by asking:

- In what ways does this passage speak to the issue of prejudice attitudes and actions?

Option 2

Read James 2:1-13.

- Think about your definition of favoritism. Do you think your definition is different from James' definition?
- Are prejudice and favoritism the same thing? Why, or why not?

James used the scenario of a rich person and a poor person visiting a synagogue as an example of favoritism.

- Why do you think James used a situation like this as his example?
- Is this type of favoritism common today? If so, how?
- Besides the rich and poor, what other situations could we substitute for the one James used?
- How is the "royal law" a contrast to favoritism?
- Why is favoritism considered a "sin" and those who show favoritism considered "lawbreakers?"
- Why is mercy an important characteristic of a follower of Christ?
- How does mercy triumph over judgment?
- How might the truths of this passage be applied to the issue of prejudice?

OPENING OUR HEARTS

Option 1

Based on today's discussion, ask your group to respond to the following questions:

- **How can we identify prejudice in our church? community? personal lives?**
- **What should our response be to acts of prejudice in our community? What about within our church?**
- **How can we overcome feelings of prejudice in our personal lives?**

Then ask the group to consider the following silently to themselves:

- **Is there anyone that I have been prejudiced against?**
- **What steps must I take to overcome these feelings?**
- **I would like God to help me with feelings of prejudice by . . .**

Option 2

Many in your group may have not thought about whether or not they have feelings of prejudice. Ask them to consider the following:

- **Do I stereotype groups of people before I know or understand them?**
- **Do I say and do things that perpetuate prejudice?**
- **Do I judge people based on outward appearance and my preconceived ideas?**

- **Do I try to see and understand others as they really are and not as I perceive them to be?**
- **Am I open to allowing God to open my eyes to see people as He sees them?**

Imaginative Option

Give each person in the class a 3" x 5" index card. Encourage each person to carry the card with them during the week and write down any examples of prejudice they observe. At the end of the week, ask them to look over the card and think about the examples they have written down. Then urge them to pray, asking God to help them be more sensitive to prejudice thoughts and actions in their lives.

Connect

WEEK 3

Weighing Facts with Our Thumb on the Scales

THIS WEEK: We know prejudice exists in the world, but does it exist in our churches? This week we will look at how and why prejudice exists and ways in which we can avoid prejudice thoughts, feelings, and actions, and allow God's grace to flow through our lives.

THINK ABOUT THIS: Have I ever been guilty of prejudice attitudes or actions?

PRAYER CONCERNS:

SAINTS AND SEX
(A CHRISTIAN PERSPECTIVE ON SEXUAL SIN)

- -

Focus Scripture: 1 Corinthians 6:12-20

Session Goal: To help students gain a godly perspective on sex.

- -

OPENING OUR MINDS

Option 1

Ask your group: **How is sexuality portrayed in our culture through the following:**

Television
Magazines
Music
Fashion

- **How is the topic of sexuality dealt with in the church?**
- **Where do culture and the church agree when it comes to the topic of sexuality? Where do they differ?**

Option 2

Ask your group to respond to the following statements.
—*"Sex is a gift from God."*
—*"Sexual desire is a normal and natural feeling."*
—*"Sex should be expressed by two people who love each other."*
—*"Only actions can be sexually immoral."*
—*"Sex is a topic that shouldn't be discussed in the church."*

Follow up by asking:

- **How is the subject of sex dealt with outside the church?**

- How should the church deal with the subject of sexual sin?
- Why is this topic so difficult for the church to discuss?

Imaginative Option

Read the following scenarios and ask the class to respond:

Bob and Mary are coworkers. Both married to other people. Recently they have been working together on a project. Since the project began, they have discovered they have a lot in common and have become close friends. Yesterday Bob and Mary went to lunch together, alone. When Bob arrived home that evening his wife, as she always does, asked how his day went and what he did for lunch. Bob told her where he went for lunch but did not mention Mary in fear that his wife might not approve. He sees his friendship with Mary as harmless and decides to keep silent about their relationship.

- **If you were Bob's friend, what advice would you give him?**

Tom and Gina have been dating for nearly two years. Recently Tom proposed to Gina and she accepted. Up to this point they have not been sexually intimate, but since their engagement they have found themselves wanting to be more physical. Both are beginning to feel guilty and confused about all that their thinking and feeling.

- **If Tom and Gina came to you for counsel, what would you say to help them in this situation?**

Mike and Lori are a couple who enjoy going to the movies. In conversation with friends, a certain movie was highly recommended. Mike and Lori always check a Christian web site that reviews movies and its content. Upon reading the review of the recommended movie, Mike discovers that this film contains a lot of sexual content, which includes nudity. All the Hollywood reviewers are giving this movie much praise and it is breaking box office records.

- **If you were Mike and Lori, would you go to the movie?**

Follow up by asking:

- **Do you think most people in our culture would respond to each situation the same way as you? Why, or why not?**

OPENING THE WORD

Understanding 1 Corinthians 6:12-20

1 Corinthians is a letter by Paul to the church at Corinth. This city was the last stop for Paul on his second missionary journey (Acts 18:1-8). Corinth was a city plagued with immoral behavior; some of this had found its way into the church. Among other issues that had inundated the church, Paul addressed the problem of immoral behavior among its members.

It is apparent that some in the church had latched onto the phrase "everything is permissible," and used it to live however they wanted. They believed because Christ had forgiven their sins they were free to do whatever they pleased. Paul reminded them of Christ's sacrifice and that they no longer lived for themselves, but for Christ. Their bodies belonged to Christ and each person was a holy temple where the Holy Spirit resided. Sexual immorality degraded that temple (their bodies) and rendered it unusable for bringing honor to God. Paul was making it clear that what we do with our bodies matters to God.

Option 1

Read 1 Corinthians 6:12-20.

- **What do you think Paul meant by** *"everything is permissible for me, but not everything is beneficial?"*
- **What do you think Paul meant by** *"the body is not meant for sexual immorality, but for the Lord, and the Lord for the body?"*
- **Do we have the right and freedom to do whatever we want with our bodies? Why, or why not?**
- **Paul says we are to "flee" from sexual immorality. One translation says we are to "run" from it. Why would Paul use a word like "flee" or "run?"**

- **How is our body a "temple of the Holy Spirit?"**
- **How can we "honor God with our bodies?" How does sexual immorality dishonor God?**
- **What does it mean that we belong to God and not to ourselves?**

Option 2

Read 1 Corinthians 6:12-20. Then, share with the group this definition of freedom: *"the ability to act freely; a state in which somebody is able to act and live as he or she chooses, without being subject to any undue restraints or restriction."*[3]

We have certain freedoms. We are free to express our opinions, live where we want, and so on. Yet, we are not totally free to do whatever we want.

- **What freedoms do we have as Christians?**
- **Are we free to do whatever we want? If not, why?**
- **What does Paul have to say about our freedoms when it comes to our bodies?**
- **How does sexual immorality make it impossible to live as a "temple of the Holy Spirit?"**
- **How do we live in such a way that our bodies honor God?**

---

3. http://encarta.msn.com/dictionary_1861613380/freedom.html. Accessed June 20, 2008.

Imaginative Option
Read 1 Corinthians 6:12-20. Give each person a pen/pencil and a piece of paper. Ask each person to write down their interpretation of 1 Corinthians 6:12, *"Everything is permissible, but not everything is beneficial."* When everyone has had a chance to write, ask for several volunteers to share their response. Follow up by discussing, as a group, how this verse relates to the overall message of 1 Corinthians 6:12-20.

OPENING OUR HEARTS

Option 1

Ask the group to get silent before God. As everyone is in an attitude of prayer, ask the group to consider these questions quietly to themselves.

- **Are there relationships for which I need God's help to set boundaries?**
- **Are there things I am watching that I need God's help to avoid?**
- **Do I have thoughts and desires that require God's purifying touch?**
- **I need God to help me keep sexually pure by . . .**

Option 2

Listed below are steps to keeping sexually pure. Read the steps aloud and ask the group to consider silently one thing they can do this week to accomplish each particular step.

1. **Focus on God**
2. **Practice self-control**
3. **Establish boundaries**
4. **Be alert**

Connect

WEEK 4

Saints and Sex

THIS WEEK: God created us with the ability for thoughts, feelings, and desires. If we allow them to, these thoughts, feelings, and desires can turn from what God intended into something corrupted by sin. This week's study will helps us get a proper perspective on sex and examine ways we can resist the temptation that leads people to fall into the trap of sexual sin.

THINK ABOUT THIS: What is my view of sexual sin?

PRAYER CONCERNS:

BEHIND CLOSED DOORS (ABUSE)

Focus Scriptures: Colossians 3:12-17; Ephesians 4:25-32

Session Goal: To help students understand that abuse is a problem both inside and outside the church.

Teacher: This lesson deals with the sensitive issue of abuse. Keep in mind that some in your class may have been, or are currently, victims of abuse. Also, you may have people in attendance who themselves are the abuser. Be prepared for possible questions and responses that might arise due to the serious nature of this lesson.

OPENING OUR MINDS

Option 1:

Ask your group whether they feel each of the following statements are examples of abuse. If they feel it is an example of abuse, follow up by asking what type of abuse is being represented by the statement.

- **One spouse, in anger, gives the other spouse the silent treatment.**
- **A boss belittles an employee in front of coworkers.**
- **A church member deliberately spreads a rumor about another church member.**
- **A grade school student is physically pushed around daily by another student.**
- **A parent spanks his or her child for misbehaving.**
- **A customer yells at a cashier in the check-out line.**

OPENING THE WORD

Understanding Colossians 3:12-17

The first chapter of Colossians speaks of the supremacy of Christ and Paul's labors for the church. The second chapter talks about the dangers of false teachers. In chapter 3, Paul focuses on Christian behavior. Verse 12 begins with "as God's chosen people . . . clothe yourselves with. . ." Followers must clothe, or "put on," the example of Christ and live a life of compassion, kindness, humility, and so on—these are the characteristics of the godly life. We must "put on" forgiveness—forgiving as the Lord forgives. We must "put on" love—this holds everything together. Without love, forgiveness and kindness are not truly possible.

Putting on the peace of God replaces the chaos of the world. This peace is the kind that only God can give and brings about harmony and unity within the body of Christ. Along with the "peace of God," Paul admonishes the church to "let the word of Christ dwell" within them. This means allowing God's Word to guide and direct their lives. Whatever they did in both word and action, they were to do in the name of Jesus.

Our attitudes and actions toward others should be like Christ, motivated by love—allowing the peace and Word of God to guide our lives.

Understanding Ephesians 4:25-32

Paul gives two warnings in verses 26-27: don't let the sun go down on your anger and do not give the devil a foothold. Angry emotions can lead to angry actions. If we do get angry, it must not lead to sin.

Our actions should not be sinful, neither should our speech. Paul says that our speech should build up and benefit those who listen. He is warning the church to guard their speech and be careful how they talk. What we say has an impact on others— both inside and outside the church. When our talk is "unwholesome," we grieve (or distress) the Holy Spirit. As one commentator puts it, "the Holy Spirit, who indwells believers and who gives himself freely to them in love, is deeply wounded whenever such irreverent and destructive talk is permitted."[4]

The life before Christ is filled with bitterness, rage, anger, and so on. Paul admonishes those who call themselves Christians to rid themselves of such things. If these remain within a believer, it hinders their relationship with God and others. Our former life must be forsaken, and kindness and forgiveness must replace those emotions and attitudes that are barriers to a Christlike life.

Option 1

Divide the group in half. On a 3" x 5" index card, write the Group number (1 or 2), Scripture passage, and questions for that particular group. Then, instruct each group to read their passage and discuss the group questions.

Group 1: Colossians 3:12-17

- **What does it mean to clothe ourselves with compassion, kindness, gentleness, and patience?**
- **Why is forgiveness so important to the Christian life?**
- **How does forgiveness relate to what Paul says in verse 12?**
- **How does love bind all things in perfect unity?**
- **Why must peace *rule* and God's Word *dwell* within our hearts?**

4. Taylor, Willard, ed. *Beacon Bible Commentary, Vol. 9* (Kansas City: Beacon Hill Press, 1965), p. 225.

- Why should everything we do, in word and deed, be done in the name of Jesus?

Group 2: Ephesians 4:25-32

- According to verse 27, is it wrong to be angry?
- What do you think it means to "not let the sun go down while you are still angry?"
- How can unresolved anger give the devil a foothold?
- How does unwholesome talk tear others down?
- What kind of speech builds people up?
- Why is it important for us to get rid of bitterness, rage, anger, brawling, slander, and malice?
- What is the power of forgiveness? (v. 32)

When each group is finished discussing, have the groups come together and share what they discovered from their passage.

Option 2

Read Colossians 3:12-17.

- What does clothing ourselves with compassion, kindness, humility, gentleness, and patience look like? Are these easy to wear?
- How does forgiveness help us in our relationship with others?
- How does having the peace of Christ rule our hearts help us in our relationship with others?
- How does letting the Word of Christ dwell in us and doing everything in the name of the Lord Jesus help us in our relationship with others?
- Do you think putting the words of this passage into practice helps us avoid abusive behavior toward others? If so, how?
- How can the message of this passage help us minister to a person who is a victim of abuse?

Read Ephesians 4:25-32.

- **How does speaking truthfully help us in our relationship with others?**
- **Why is it important not to sin when we get angry?**
- **Why is avoiding unwholesome talk important in our relationship with others?**
- **How can bitterness, rage, anger, brawling, slander, and malice effect our lives?**
- **Why do you think Paul specifically mentions being kind, compassionate, and forgiving toward others?**
- **Do you think putting the words of this passage into practice helps us avoid abusive behavior toward others? If so, how?**
- **How can the message of this passage help us minister to a person who is a victim of abuse?**

OPENING OUR HEARTS

Option 1

Summarize the story of Tom (located in the Participant's Guide, Chapter 5). Ask the group to consider the following questions silently.

- **How might God use you to minister to someone who has experienced abuse?**
- **How might God use you to minister to someone who is responsible for the abuse of another?**

Close in prayer:

- *Pray* that God will help the group become more sensitive to those who have experienced abuse.
- *Pray* for God's comfort, guidance, and direction for those who are currently being abused or have experienced abuse in the past.

- *Pray* that God will speak to the hearts of everyone in the group, making them aware of any possible abusive words or actions they may be committing toward another.

Option 2

Ask the group to consider the following silently.

- **How can I clothe myself with compassion, kindness, humility, gentleness, and patience this week?**
- **What is one way I can practice forgiveness in my life?**
- **Am I allowing the peace of Christ to rule in my heart?**
- **How can the "word of Christ dwell" more fully in my life?**
- **Am I doing everything, in word and deed, in the name of Jesus?**

Close by reciting the Lord's Prayer (Matthew 6:9-13) as a group.

Connect -

WEEK 5

Behind Closed Doors

THIS WEEK: Most people have experienced some form of abuse in their life. Without us even knowing it, the people we interact with each day may have been, or are currently, victims of abuse. This week we will examine the topic of abuse and what the Bible has to say about this serious issue.

THINK ABOUT THIS: What do I consider abuse?

PRAYER CONCERNS:

DON'T GET HOOKED (ADDICTIONS)

Focus Scripture: Exodus 20:1–6

Session Goal: To help students understand that people can be addicted to more than just drugs, alcohol, or gambling.

OPENING OUR MINDS

Option 1

Ask your group whether they *Agree or Disagree* with each of the following statements.

- **Addiction is a dependency on a behavior or substance in which a person is helpless to stop.**
- **An addiction to food, power, or possessions can be just as devastating as being addicted to drugs or alcohol.**
- **A person who has an addiction is easy to identify.**
- **People who suffer from an addiction need help beyond themselves.**
- **Addictions are easy to overcome.**
- **Christians are not susceptible to addictions.**
- **All addictions are harmful.**

Option 2

Substance addiction is where a person is dependent on a substance. **Ask your group to name substances people can be addicted to.**

Process addiction is where a person is addicted to a certain behavior. **Ask your group to name behaviors people can be addicted to.**

Ask,

- **How do people become addicted?**
- **Are addictions easy to overcome? Why, or why not?**
- **Can a Christian suffer from addiction?**
- **Are there any addictions that might be considered harmless or acceptable?**

OPENING THE WORD

Understanding Exodus 20:1-6

Moses encountered God at Mt. Sinai. During that meeting with the divine, Moses received what we have to come to call the Ten Commandments. These commands are introduced, in verse 2, by God's declaration to the people that He was *their* God. He alone brought them out of slavery. He alone was to be their God. He alone was to be the object of their worship.

Once God established His authority, He gave the first command: "You shall have no other gods before me." The word "*before*" in this verse means "side by side" or "in addition." God was saying He would not share the affection of people (then and now) with any god, person, place, or thing. There is no room for competitors when it comes to our relationship with God.

The second command, in verses 4-6, prohibits people from worshipping idols. The people were warned not to bow down to anything other than God. He is a "jealous God," and there-

DON'T GET HOOKED

37

fore the devotion of the people must be to Him only. God was making it clear that nothing in our lives can have more of our love, affection, or devotion than we have for Him.

It is no accident that the first two commands have to do with our relationship with God. He must be the center of our worship and the focus of our life. This means loving and serving Him only; not allowing anything to take priority over Him in our thoughts, feelings, or actions.

Option 1

Begin by asking:

- **How would you define the word "idol?"**
- **What might be considered an idol today?**

Read Exodus 20:1-6. Then, ask the following questions:

- **Why do you think God reminds them of who He is (vv. 1-2) before giving them the commandments?**
- **How would you interpret the phrase "no other gods before me" in verse 3?**
- **What does it mean to bow down to something other than to God?**
- **If God is a "jealous God," how might our actions provoke His jealousy?**
- **How would you explain the message of these verses to someone who had never read (or heard) them before?**

Option 2

Begin by asking the group: **What image comes to mind when you hear the word *idol*?**

Read Exodus 20:1-6.

- **Compare a "god" during the time of Moses to now?**

- What might an idol look like during the time of Moses?
- What does an idol look like today?
- What did bowing to an idol look like then? What does bowing to an idol look like now?
- Why does the worship and bowing to anything other than God make Him jealous?
- Why is it important that we make God the only object of our worship?

Imaginative Option

Show a picture of someone bowing. Ask: **What thoughts come to your mind when you see this picture?** Then, read Exodus 20:1-6 and ask the group to respond to the following:

- **Give an example of someone bowing down to money.**
- **Give an example of someone bowing down to material possessions.**
- **Give an example of someone bowing down to food.**
- **Give an example of someone bowing down to power.**
- **Give an example of someone bowing down to God.**
- **Why does God command that we bow down to no one other than Him?**

OPENING OUR HEARTS

Option 1

Share the following definitions[5]:

A god—a representation of a god, used as an object of worship.
Idol—somebody or something greatly admired or loved, often to excess.
Addiction—great interest in a particular thing to which a lot of time is devoted.

Using these definitions, ask the group to answer the following questions silently.

- **When it comes to my material possessions, do I treat any or all of them as a god or idol?**
- **Is there a relationship in my life that might be considered a god, idol, or addiction?**
- **Do I participate in an activity that might fit the definition of addiction?**
- **Is there anyone or anything in my life that might cause God to be jealous?**
- **With God's help, one thing I can do this week to avoid idol worship in my life is . . .**

Option 2

An idol is not just a giant statue. We can bow down and worship a possession, a person, or activity. God's command is that we worship Him alone. Nothing in our lives should take priority over our relationship with Him.

Ask:

- **How can we avoid the worship of people?**
- **How can we avoid the worship of possessions?**
- **How can we avoid the worship of activities?**
- **How can we avoid the misuse of power?**

5. <http://encarta.msn.com/dictionary_1861614461/god.html>. Accessed July 2, 2008

- **How can we recognize when someone or something has become an idol or addiction in our life?**

Connect _

WEEK 6

Don't Get Hooked

THIS WEEK: We are quick to identify the most common addictions people suffer with such as alcohol, drugs, and gambling. However, are there acceptable addictions that we seem to ignore? This week we will explore things in our lives that might be considered addictions, how they affect our lives, and how God can help us gain control over these areas.

THINK ABOUT THIS: Do I have anything in my life that might be considered an addiction?

PRAYER CONCERNS:

IS GOD A DEMOCRAT OR REPUBLICAN? (POLITICS)

Focus Scripture: Joshua 5:13—6:5

Session Goal: To help students understand that God has no political affiliation.

OPENING OUR MINDS

Option 1

Read each quote below without sharing who the author is or this person's political affiliation. Ask the group to respond as to whether they think the quote was spoken by a Democrat or Republican. After they respond, reveal who said it and what political party the person is, or was, affiliated with.

> *"Be a listener only, keep within yourself, and endeavor to establish with yourself the habit of silence, especially in politics."* —Thomas Jefferson (Democratic-Republican Party)

> *"Don't sacrifice your political convictions for the convenience of the hour."* —Edward M. Kennedy (Democrat)

> *"Character is like a tree and reputation like its shadow. The shadow is what we think of it; the tree is the real thing."* —Abraham Lincoln (Republican)

> *"Human rights is the soul of our foreign policy, because human rights is the very soul of our sense of nationhood."* —Jimmy Carter (Democrat)

Follow up by asking:

- **Can you tell by just looking at someone what political party they belong to? Why, or why not?**
- **Are most people vocal about their political views? Why, or why not?**
- **How do people decide their political affiliation?**

- **Should people belong to a political party or be involved in the political process?**

Option 2

Most people think "Republican" or "Democrat" when it comes to a political party. However, in the United States there at least five (*Republican, Democratic, Libertarian, Constitution,* and *Green Party*).

Ask:

- **What is the purpose of a political party?**
- **How do people choose a political party?**
- **Should Christians be involved in politics? Why, or why not?**
- **Is it always easy to know which candidate to support? Why, or why not?**
- **How do people determine how to vote on an issue?**

Imaginative Option

Display a map of the world.

- **What are the dangers of thinking God is on your side because of where you live?**

Display a picture of the Democrat (donkey) and Republican (elephant) party symbols.

- **Are there any dangers in thinking God is on your side because of the political party you are affiliated with?**

Follow up by asking:

- **Does ever God favor one country, political party, or culture over another? Why, or why not?**

OPENING THE WORD

Understanding Joshua 5:13—6:5

The setting for this passage takes place just before Joshua and the Israelites entered Jericho. Joshua, the leader of this army, encountered "a man standing with a drawn sword" (v. 13). Joshua asked the man whose side he was on. The answer "neither" by the commander of the Lord's army is important for us to understand. God is not on *our* side, but we are called to be on *His* side. The battle Joshua was about to enter was not Joshua's, it was God's.

The commander of the Lord asked Joshua to remove his sandals for he was standing on holy ground. Taking your sandals off was a sign of respect and submission. Joshua obeyed, indicating that he had understood the importance of this encounter. The Lord revealed to Joshua that He had already "delivered Jericho" into his hands. God told Joshua what to do to secure the city and win the battle. We see in the proceeding verses (Joshua 6:6-27) that Joshua obeyed and defeated the enemy.

Option 1

Begin by sharing a paraphrased version of the battle of Jericho (Joshua 6:6-27). Follow up by telling the group that the story you are about to read took place prior to the battle. Then, read Joshua 5:13-15.

- **Why do you think Joshua asked the man with the drawn sword "are you for us or for our enemies?"**
- **Do you think Joshua's question was the right one to ask? Why, or why not?**
- **Are you surprised by the answer the commander of the Lord's army gives to Joshua? What does the commander's answer "neither" tell us about the battle?**

- What does Joshua's response in verses 14-15 tell us about his faith in God?

Read Joshua 6:1-5.

- Why was it important for Joshua to listen to the Lord and obey His instructions?
- Why is it important for us to listen to the Lord and obey His instructions?
- Was the battle Joshua's or the Lord's?
- Is there a difference between believing "God is on our side" and "we are on God's side?"

Option 2

Begin by asking:

- What is the danger of believing "God is on our side" as opposed to understanding that we are to be "on God's side?"
- Have you ever made a big decision without seeking God's wisdom and direction?

Read Joshua 5:13—6:5. Share with the group that this story takes place prior to the battle of Jericho (Joshua 6:6-27).

- What does this story tell us about Joshua?
- What does this story tell us about God?
- What does this story tell us about listening to God and following His direction?

Imaginative Option

Play the Veggie Tales video *Josh and the Big Wall!* This is a funny and unique way to tell the story of Joshua and the Battle of Jericho (Joshua 6:6-27). Following the video, read Joshua 5:13—6:5. Explain that this story takes place prior to the battle. Discuss the message and meaning of this story in light of the Jericho battle.

OPENING OUR HEARTS

Option 1

Read Acts 10:34 and Romans 2:11. Share with the group that these two verses point to the fact that God shows no favoritism. He is not for some groups and against others. God does not choose sides; rather, He wants us to choose Him and His ways.

- **How do Acts 10:34 and Romans 2:11 relate to today's discussion on political parties?**

Ask your group to think about these questions as each person quiets his or her heart before God.

- **Do I align myself with God and His ways, or do I expect God to align himself with me and my ways?**
- **Do I make decisions in light of Scripture, or do I listen more to popular opinion?**
- **Am I listening to the guidance and direction of the Holy Spirit to guide my thoughts, beliefs, and actions?**

Option 2

Read the quote from Tony Campolo. "God *'stands above all political parties and calls each of them into judgment. Likewise, He calls upon us to rise above all of this, and He expects us to use the Scriptures as a touchstone to test whether the policies and practices of political parties are in harmony with His will.'*"[6]

Regardless of political party, we must always follow God and obey Him above anything else. The truth is that God is not on the side of any particular political party. The question is not whether God is on our side, but are we on God's side? The key is to focus on God and His Word for guidance.

6. Campolo, Tony. *Is Jesus A Republican or a Democrat?* (Dallas: Word Publishing, Co., 1995), p. 3.

Close by discussing ways in which we can rise above political parties and make a difference in the world for Christ.

Connect

WEEK 7

Is God a Democrat or Republican?

THIS WEEK: The majority of people align themselves with a particular political party. The reality is that politics has a profound impact on our lives, but is something rarely discussed in church. This week we will discuss how we can develop a biblical worldview when it comes to politics.

THINK ABOUT THIS: Is there one political party that God favors? Why, or why not?

PRAYER CONCERNS: